GUN CONTROL LAWS IN US

The United States is known to have the maximum amount of privately owned guns (about 200 million) than any other country or state. Every year, about 640,000 crimes occur, and out of that murder crimes rise to 16,000 annually. Thus the high rate of private gun ownership is a highly debated topic they are living in the US or abroad.

The founding fathers of the United states believed that armed citizens would be an asset to the country as citizen militias were considered an important part of the country's defense.

The Second Amendment states :

- "A well regulated Militia, being necessary to the security of a free State, the right of the people to keep and bear Arms, shall not be infringed."

Over the years, legislation to restrict the availability of firearms to the public has brought up these issues: What restrictions on firearms are permissible under the Constitution? Does gun control constitute crime control? One key difference of opinion among legal experts is whether or not the two clauses of the second amendment are linked or not.

1) A well regulated Militia, being necessary to the security of a free State,

2) The right of the people to keep and bear Arms, shall not be infringed."

Until 2008, most legal interpretations maintained that these were linked. However in 2008 District of Columbia v. Heller , the US Supreme court ruled that these clauses were separate. D.C. Law restricted residents from owning handguns and that all firearms should be kept unloaded and locked.

The court, in a 5-4 ruling, ruled that the "Second Amendment guarantees an individual right to possess a firearm unconnected with service in a militia and to use that arm for traditionally lawful purposes, such as self-defense within the home." It was considered to be one of the most important rulings in the Second Amendment history and has been frequently used as precedence in lower court rulings.

Most gun control advocates emphasize that the clauses are linked but most gun rights advocated maintain that they are not. . The debate has been intense. To gun control activists, the opposition is out of touch with the times, misunderstands the Second Amendment, and does not care for bloodshed that guns cause. Their opponents on the other hand think that their activism is based on sheer thoughtlessness and lack of understanding of the country's issues, bent on disarming the American citizen and moved by irrational hostility toward gun enthusiasts

Can the nation's rates of homicide, robbery, and assault be reduced by the stricter regulation of firearms commerce or ownership? Would restrictions stop attacks on public figures or thwart deranged persons and terrorists?

US citizens have clashing views when it comes to gun control laws. Some believe that gun control laws can lower the crime rate. While others say that such laws should be less strict as they help protect US citizens. The severity, availability, and freedom to use firearms must be checked. This must be done for the reduction of accidents caused by the illegal use of guns or mishandling.

In the beginning, Americans used guns for not only hunting food but for protection and recreational purposes. Soon enough as gun manufacturing and popularity grew, handguns were considered an essential part of everyday life. Young boys were trained to properly use guns to provide food and security to their families. In the South, free from the restrictions of the northern colonies, hunting came to be enjoyed for the sport as well as the meat. The significance of firearms can be seen through the way Americans adapt themselves to different circumstances. For example, the Kentucky rifle was developed due to environmental demands. It was easy to carry with a long barrel which helped to hunt animals for food i.e. squirrels.

Americans gradually developed better performing weapons such as buffalo rifle according to their needs.

The first gun control law that was adopted in the New York state of America was the Sullivan act (1911). It was followed in New York because of the rising crime rates. According to this law, a person must obtain a permit to possess a handgun. The Sullivan Act was passed when America was becoming an urban nation. As the concept of rural America was getting old, people living in urban areas gradually started considering guns as a weapon of violence. Guns were no longer considered normal tools for sports. It was the time when awareness regarding the importance of gun control laws was spread.

Firearms were subject to several restrictions even in colonial days. Laws included banning the sale of guns to Native Americans and banning slaves from owning guns.

The decade of 1930 is considered important for its association with the two significant federal gun control laws.

The national firearm act 1934 and the federal firearms act in 1938. These laws didn't affect the rights of law abiding citizens to own handguns.

AS the rate of organized crimes increased in the late twenties and early thirties, the efforts to disarm the criminals also increased.

The uniform firearm act was passed in 1931 in New York. It was signed by Governor Franklin D. Roosevelt as a replacement for the Sullivan act.

Both the control acts of the 1930s were considered effective as they didn't target the law-abiding citizens but aimed at disarming the criminals.

The period of 1940 to 1960 was considered less strict in terms of gun control laws. This was because of the Second World War, the Korean War, and the cold war that it appeared inappropriate to obstruct the right of gun ownership.

1960 was marked as the decade where a lot of violence and political disturbance took place. This is the reason stricter gun control laws were made. The 1960s were marked as the decade when the first federal gun control law was adopted.

In the 1970s most of the gun control laws were focusing on the handguns. The growing number of gun sale in the 1970's show that majority of the US citizens were not comfortable relying entirely on the police for protection.

On Apr. 27, 2020, the US Supreme Court indicated it would not rule on New York State Rifle & Pistol Association Inc. et al., v. City of New York. The case revolved around a New York City regulation that prevented residents with "premises licenses" to take their guns to second homes and shooting ranges outside of New York City. The city repealed the regulation when the US Supreme Court agreed to hear the case.

Federal Regulation of Gun control

The general use and possession of guns is regulated by the National Firearms Act of 1934 and the Gun Control Act of 1968, as amended. Many state gun control laws are considered stricter than federal laws. For example, for gun transfers, some states have laws that require permits to possess guns. Moreover, some state gun laws require a particular waiting period.

The National Firearms Act (NFA)

Initially, the main objective of NFA was to make gun possession (machine guns and short-barreled guns) difficult for gangsters. This law regulates the use of guns, other than pistols and revolvers, like cane, pen, and belt buckle guns. The law imposes taxes and requires registration with the Attorney general on the production and distribution of firearms.

The Gun Control Act of 1968 (GCA)

The GCA states that the purpose behind the federal regulation of gun control is to help the law enforcement at the federal, state, and local levels. The main objective behind this is to reduce violence and crime rates. The GCA also states that they do not intend to make unnecessary laws or burden the citizens regarding the use of guns for recreational purposes. This includes hunting, target shooting, and self-defense, etc.

Amendments were made in the GCA. It includes federal restrictions on domestic commerce in ammunition and small arm. It requires the manufacturing, distribution, and all the general firearm business to be licensed by the federation. It doesn't allow the mail delivery of firearms within the state. It generally prohibits the sale of guns within the state and to people like:

- Underage individuals
- People with previous criminal records

It also makes it the responsibility of the attorney general to prohibit the import of non-sporting guns. The amendments also make it clear that the dealers must maintain the records of gun sales. There are penalties for the use of guns

in the crime of violence and the drug trafficking crimes.

According to the amendments by the Brady Handgun Violence Prevention Act, 1993, the GCA makes it mandatory to complete the background checks for unlicensed persons who want to buy guns from federal firearm licensees.

The original Brady legislation was introduced in 1988, but was not signed into law until November 30, 1993, by President Bill Clinton. The 1993 Brady Handgun Violence Prevention Act established a federal requirement for background checks for handgun purchasers and applied to licensed sellers of handguns, including licensed importers, dealers, and manufacturers.

President Obama announced new executive actions on gun control in the January of 2016. They consisted of expansion of background checks (closing the "gun show loophole"); the addition of 200 ATF agents; increased mental health care funding as well as $4 million and personnel to enhance the National Integrated

Ballistics Information Network (used to link crimes in one jurisdiction to ballistics evidence in another) and creating an Internet Investigations Center to track illegal online gun trafficking. They also included a new Department of Health and Human Services rule saying that it is not a HIPAA violation to report mental health information to the background check system and a new requirement to report gun thefts.

Gun Enthusiasts Favoring the gun control measures

For years, gun control laws supporters and opponents have been debating over the currently existing and new gun control measures. Following is the list of gun control measures that is supported by the handgun enthusiasts.

Right to carry guns

In the last 30 years, gun enthusiasts have made successful attempts to make the state pass laws that allow carrying guns. At present, 4 states have not banned carrying such deadly weapons, Arizona, Vermont, Wyoming, and Alaska. The most common state gun control laws include background checks, waiting periods, and registration requirements to purchase or sell guns.

Thirty-eight states of the US follow "shall-issue" laws. According to these laws, if a person meets certain conditions, he is allowed to carry a concealed weapon. The requirements include:

- Being a state resident

- Age should be above 18 years
- The person must pass the criminal background test
- The person must attend a hand-gun safety workshop
- Paying a certain amount of fee

Ten states of the US have "may issue" laws. These laws mean that a permit can be issued if a person meets certain conditions but mostly a permit is not issued. There is this one state named Illinois, which prohibits carrying a concealed gun.

A major focus of state-level legislation was the right to carry concealed weapons. In 2019, approximately 35 states required a permit to carry concealed weapons in public. Of the 35 states, the process for permitting followed either "may issue," "limited discretion shall issue," or "no discretion shall issue." In "may issue" states, the law provided wider discretion to the issuing authority to deny permits based on failure to meet good character standards or lacking good reason to carry in public. For "shall issue" states, either some form of limited discretion was given to the issuing authority to deny permits or the issuing authority had no discretion to deny permits that met all legal requirements. Of the three dozen states, only 26 required some form of firearm training or knowledge as part of the process to receive a permit to carry.

When assault-style weapons and high-capacity magazines were used in mass shootings, they resulted in far more deaths and injuries. From 2009 to 2018, the five deadliest mass shootings in the United States all involved the use of assault-style weapons and high-capacity magazines: Las Vegas (58 deaths), Orlando (49 deaths), Newtown (27 deaths), Sutherland Springs (25 deaths), and Parkland (17 deaths).

On April 20, 1999 America witnessed one of the deadliest and one of the worst mass shootings in our history. It occurred in the town of Littleton, Colorado at Columbine Highschool.

Two students Eric Harris (18) and Dylan Klebold (17) entered their high school and proceeded to then gun down 12 classmates, one teacher, and also wound about 20 others before killing themselves. In the years following this tragedy our nation has come to see many more tragedies like this one. The number of incidents just like Columbine have been increasing instead of decreasing over the years and has prompted much debate about gun control laws and the safety of students across our nation.

Some of the prominent school shootings have occurred at Columbine High School, Virginia Tech, Sandy Hook Elementary, and most recently Stoneman Douglas High School.

Gun-enthusiasts believe that as long as they are following the laws, they are allowed to carry handguns wherever they want.

In 2010 a new federal law was passed in which people were allowed to take guns in the parks if they abide by the law. Today, a person with a permit can carry a concealed gun in most of the national parks. Most of the states put a restriction on carrying guns into places where alcohol is served like bars and nightclubs. Until recently, some states have allowed guns to be carried in such establishment i.e. restaurants and hotels serving alcohol

. Gun enthusiasts believe that they should be allowed to carry handguns because they strictly abide by the law. According to such people, carrying guns is their right in order to protect themselves. Whereas criminals will carry guns wherever they want because they are ignorant towards state laws. The other category of people are the opponents who believe that a large number of people carrying guns means an increase in crime rates and deaths

Measures to control Gun violence

Supporters of gun control laws believe that the Second Amendment to the Constitution, is being misread in today's modern society. They contend that the Second Amendment

(a) is now outdated, with the presence of professional police forces;

(b) was intended only to guard against suppression of state militias by the central government

(c) does not guarantee a right that is absolute, but rather one that can be limited by reasonable requirements. They ask why in today's modern society a private citizen needs any firearm that is not designed primarily for hunting or other recognized sporting purposes.

Lately, they argue that only federal laws can be effective in the United States because states with few restrictions will continue to be sources of guns that flow illegally into more-restrictive states.

Gun enthusiasts are against several gun control laws which are favored by supporters of gun control laws.

- Firearm license

Gun enthusiasts believe that in order to keep the guns away from wrong hands licenses should be provided to gun owners just the way car owners get their licenses.

Opponents disagree with this idea. According to them, gun ownership must not be compared with cars, as owning a car is a luxury not a right.

- Safety devices

Smart guns with built-in locks can only be used by lawful owners. Supporters of this gun control measure believe that it will prevent others or unlawful individuals to operate the guns. Opponents think that this idea is costly and might be unconstitutional.

- Serial numbers

Putting serial numbers on the bullets helps to identify and helps to keep them in the record. Supporters think that bullets are often found and can be identified to solve a particular crime. Opponents of such gun control measures believe that criminals can remove such serial numbers. According to them, it will only increase the cost burden on all the buyers.

- Limit the gun purchases

Much of the illegal trade of guns is mostly done by middlemen who then further sell the firearms to gangsters. Supporters of this law believe that it will stop the illegal trade of guns. Opponents think that this law is ineffective as the middlemen will use other means to get the guns.

Eligibility for gun possession

According to the current gun control law, following people are restricted from possessing, transferring, or receiving firearms.

- Persons who have committed a crime and who have been punished imprisonment for a time period of more than a year
- Escapees
- Firearm users who are unlawful or drug addicts
- Persons suffering from any mental illness or mentally defective individuals
- Immigrants who are unauthorized and nonimmigrant visitors
- People who have been disgracefully discharged from the u.s. armed forces;
- People who have abandoned their u.s. citizenship;

- Persons who have been charged for assaulting, threatening, and stalking their close partners or child of their partners
- Persons who have been charged for domestic violence

The NRA has been a huge supporter of gun rights in the US. While the NRA was the standard-bearer for gun rights advocacy, numerous other groups followed in its footsteps to lobby for Second Amendment protections, organize at the grassroots level, and raise money for political candidates who supported their causes. Total campaign contributions during 1990-2018 for gun rights were estimated to be $42.1 million. Total outside spending for gun rights during 2010-2018 was estimated at $113.6 million. On Jan. 15, 2021, the NRA filed for bankruptcy, and announced plans to leave New

York and move to Texas where the organization will reincorporate. New York Attorney General Letitia James called the move a "tactic to evade accountability and my office's oversight."

Age Eligibility

Federal firearms licensees are not allowed to transfer a long gun and handgun to people who are under 18 and less than 21 respectively. Since 1994, it is considered unlawful for an unlicensed individual to transfer a handgun to a person who is under 18. Thus it is illegal for an under 18 to possess a gun with the exception of employment, hunting and target practice, etc.

Michigan Gun Laws

State of Michigan Constitution

- <u>Article 1 Section 6</u> – Every person has the right to keep and bear arms for the defense of himself and the State. (1963 MI Const.)

In some states such as Michigan <u>carrying a non-concealed firearm is generally legal.</u> Officers may engage in a consensual encounter with a person carrying a non-concealed pistol; however, <u>in order to stop a citizen, officers are required to have reasonable suspicion that crime is afoot. For example, officers may not stop a person on the mere possibility the person may be carrying an unregistered pistol.</u>

Some believe that owning a firearm can deter crime.

- 44 states allow some type of Open Carry of a handgun.

- 6 states ban Open Carry.

- The Open Carry movement is growing in the US, much like the Concealed Carry movement has in the last 10-15 years.

School shooting in the US

There is a big reason to why people call gun a deadly weapon. Apart from the recreational and protection purposes, firearms are used in horrible ways. One of the worst consequence of unlawful use of firearms is school shooting. The year 2018 was quite tragic as the most incidents of school shooting in US occurred in that year.

It is quite unfortunate to say that since 1970, America has faced 1,316 cases of school shootings. It is said that school shooting in US has risen up to 18% after the Sandy Hook Elementary School incident which took place in 2012. In US, gun shooting is one of the leading cause of deaths among children.

Dangers Associated With Firearms

Private ownership of guns is common in the US. According to most people, they own firearms for the sake of self-defense and other recreational purposes. Unfortunately, having a deadly weapon like guns give rise to suicides, accidents, and domestic violence. In the US, suicides due to firearms take the highest percentage of violent accidents. This continuously rising suicide rate is often ignored when debating over the gun control laws. The violence resulting from the unlawful use of handguns not only causes deaths, bloodshed, and an enormous amount of injuries but also portrays a negative image of a country.

Firearms have become a significant cause behind the rise of domestic violence in the US. Households possessing firearms have a femicide rate five times more than the homes without such deadly weapons. Thus Guns are horrible weapons because of their association with murder, death, and bloodshed. It is reported that many children are killed by firearms every day in the US.

The Mexican government sued US gun producers in US federal court this year in 2021. The Mexican government blamed the manufacturers, including Smith & Wesson Brands, Inc.; Barrett Firearms Manufacturing,

Inc.; Beretta U.S.A. Corp.; Colt's Manufacturing Company LLC, and Glock Inc, of "actively facilitating the unlawful trafficking of their guns to drug cartels and other criminals in Mexico."

When unlawful usage of firearms becomes common, crime rates increase. Hospitals and rehabilitation centers are full of victims and survivors of the shooting. Gun violence affects the economy too. The hospital or medical bills for the injured individuals are quite huge which are mostly covered by the US government. Thus, the tax system is affected along with the overall stability of the economic system. AS the annual healthcare bills due to gun violence in the US is about $4 billion which rises to $100 billion in the long term. Many laws have been passed about different subjects but the topic of gun control still remains debatable.

Ghost" guns

To compound matters, there are now gun-manufacturing rings that assemble firearms with parts obtained legally and without any serial numbers called "ghost guns." Police say 3D printers are also being used to either make guns or create parts that enable the weapon to fire more rounds at a time.

A unique solution that Canada is implementing is the buy back program. Their National buyback program pays $200 for long guns and $350 for handguns. One place police might look for gun trading is the dark web, an encrypted part of the internet where illegal sales flourish. One notable case saw a former University of Toronto philosophy student legally buy 23 handguns — 15 from a single retailer — for resale.

www.ingramcontent.com/pod-product-compliance
Lightning Source LLC
Chambersburg PA
CBHW050323220526
45465CB00005B/2101